The Art of Climbing

Contents

Written by Liz Miles

Collins

Why climb?

People climb for many reasons, whether it's to rescue, for work, to explore, as a hobby, to compete or for art. There are many different ways to climb.

Let's delve into the amazing world of climbing ...

Caution!
Climbing can be dangerous. Do not climb without special training and equipment.

Climbing for exploration

In the past, tourists sometimes climbed up structures to discover more about them.

Visitors on an ancient Egyptian pyramid in the 1890s. Today, they would be fined for climbing here!

5

Wall climbing

Some people climb on special walls in gyms.
Unlike a real rock wall, there are no crumbling
ledges or wet conditions.

thumb and fingertips grip

climbing holds

toes push off

Climbers are taught to bridge large gaps with their bodies. Look at how this climber gets his limbs into position.

knee pushed against wall

Big wall rock climbing

Big wall rock climbing needs skill and precision. Some big walls go straight up or have overhangs.

One climber – Lynn Hill – took just a day to **free climb** a well-known big wall climb in the US called The Nose.

The Nose

8

Top-rope climbing

Climbers often use safety ropes so they won't plunge to the ground if they slip.

an anchor (ring) holds the rope

a second climber controls the rope (this is called belaying)

9

Parkour

Parkour runners scale walls, do special rolls, jumps, backflips and plunges in competitions to get across a course fast.

Films often have action-packed parkour chases, with parkour experts lunging from cranes to rooftops and jumping across dizzying gaps.

Caution!
Parkour runners and stunt people make it look easy, but you must not try this without proper training!

Free running

Free running is like parkour but has more room for **self-expression**. Free runners follow their own vision, making up fancy jumps, flips and twists.

Climbing at work

Climbing is vital in lots of jobs and careers. Painters, roofers, scaffolders and window cleaners need to climb walls using ladders.

Lots of city structures are too tall for ladders! These window cleaners use suspension cables anchored to the roof to take them to each floor.

Workers need to pick the right days — it's too dangerous to do this work in windy conditions.

13

Steeplejacks climb high structures for work.
They clean, repair and restore things like chimneys.
Before climbing the ladders, they must attach
safety harnesses.

Wind turbine technicians, like Jessica Kilroy, climb very high towers. They carry weighty equipment. They can climb on to the outside walls of the **rotor** and blades.

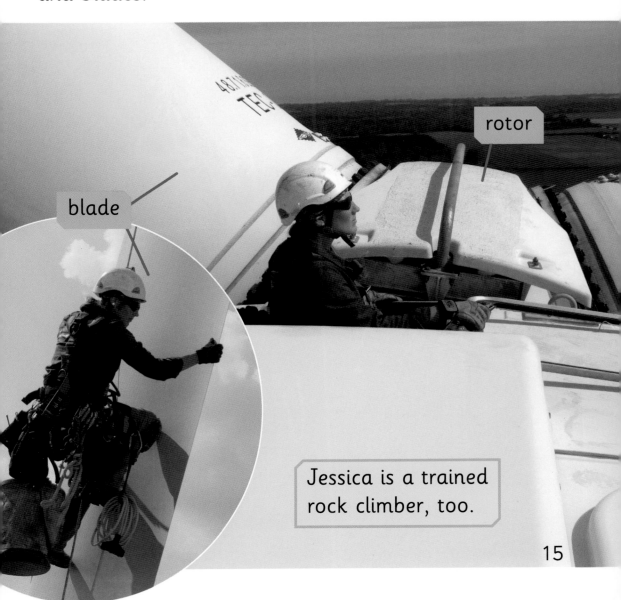

rotor

blade

Jessica is a trained rock climber, too.

Climbing to rescue

Special emergency service workers may need to climb to save rock climbers after accidents. They are taught how to get a patient down on a stretcher.

Here, a dog fell off the edge of a cliff. Trained mountain rescue volunteers had to climb down the sheer rocks to rescue it.

Climbing for art

Some artists work on a large scale and paint their art on walls, so lots of people can see it.

Kobra is a spray paint artist. He stood on a platform on cables to paint this **mural** in Brazil.

Billboard workers climb high to stick posters on walls, too.

Climb on!

Lots of people climb. Some climb for sport, art, for fun or to beat records.

Workers climb to clean and repair tall structures.

Street climbers are athletes and artists.

If you want to start climbing, try starting out on a gym wall! Learn the skills so you can climb on ... and up!

Glossary

free climb climb only using ropes to prevent falling

mural a painting or other work of art applied directly onto a wall in a public place

rotor a turning hub, like the middle of a bike wheel

self-expression show your own skills and feelings

technicians people skilled with mechanical things

wind turbine a kind of windmill that turns wind energy into electricity

Climbing for ...

exploration

hobby

sport

work

art

rescue

self-expression

competitions

23

🐾 Review: After reading 🐾

Use your assessment from hearing the children read to choose any GPCs, words or tricky words that need additional practice.

Read 1: Decoding

- Ask the children to practise reading these words with the /sh/ sound:

  technicians   **suspension**   **self-expression**   **caution**

- Ask the children to take turns to read a page aloud, as fluently as possible. Say: blend new words in your head before you read them aloud.

Read 2: Prosody

- Ask the children to read pages 10 and 11, paying attention to the punctuation. Discuss which words you'd emphasize to create excitement and the idea that parkour has an element of danger. Talk about the purpose of the exclamation in the text box and how you could convey the seriousness of training for parkour. Do they:
  - o pause at commas
  - o read hyphenated words together smoothly?

Read 3: Comprehension

- Look together at the contents page and ask the children which forms of climbing they have tried, and which they would like to try, and why.
- Discuss the Caution box on page 3. Ask: Why might all the types of climbing be dangerous in some way? Which type of climbing is the most dangerous? Discuss the importance of safety equipment.
- Point to the word **self-expression** on page 11. Ask the children for their own definition of **self-expression** and then compare it to the definition on page 21. Ask:
  - o What sort of moves might a free runner do to show their agility, or to express their hopes? (e.g. *fast flips; high jumps*)
  - o What other sports or activities show self-expression through body moves? (e.g. *ballet, breakdancing*)
- Point to the word **art** on the cover. Discuss what the children would expect from something described as an art. (e.g. it is *creative, skilled*)
- Look together at pages 22 and 23. Encourage the children to talk about the different forms of climbing and compare them. Which did they find most interesting to read about, and why?